First edition 2015

Disclaimer:

DIARY

OF A
MINECRAFT
IRON GOLEM

BOOKS KID

TABLE OF CONTENTS

Day 1

My name's Harvey. I'm an iron golem. Most people think that iron golems are really big and scary because we're so powerful. It's true that I have a strong punch, but there's nothing scary about me. I'm lovely I am and gentle as a lamb unless you do something to annoy me.

Then I'll get really angry and I'm no fun to be around when I'm angry.

I live in a village. I haven't always lived in this village. I've traveled all over Minecraftia, seen places I could never have imagined. I have even gone down to the Nether, but right now I work as a guard for a village in the west of Minecraftia.

If I'm honest, the work's very boring. Wander around the village, keep your eyes open for monsters, make sure everyone's safe. Same thing day in, day out.

The only problem is that we never get any monsters around here. I heard rumors that there were some skeletons out by the farms, but I didn't see any. So instead I spend every day

1

roaming around, trying to look like I'm doing something, when really I'm bored, bored, bored.

I used to work in a village that was under constant attack from zombies. That was fun. Every night I had to go out and smash the skeletons. I wish I hadn't left to come here, but I thought it would be nice to have a break from fighting skeletons every night.

Boy, was I wrong.

Thank goodness for my flower garden. It's the one bright thing in my day. When I've finished work, I go to my own private little place and tend to my flowers.

I've spent a lot of time making my garden just perfect. I've got all sorts of flowers there. Red ones, yellow ones, orange ones, blue ones. Whatever your favorite color, I've got a flower to suit you.

If there's a villager I think needs cheering up, I take them one of my flowers. I choose the flower I'm going give to them very carefully to make sure it's the perfect one to brighten their mood.

I think the villagers think I'm a bit odd when I give them flowers. They always stare at me for a while and then grunt. Is a little 'thank you' too much to ask?

I'm not sure that I'm going to stay in this village for much longer. I think it's time to get some excitement back in my life.

Day 2

OK, I know I said that I wanted some excitement in my life, but I didn't mean like this. Someone's been stealing my flowers! What makes it worse is that I think they've been doing it for a long time. Taking my flowers from right under my nose. It's not fair.

I had a beautiful bright red poppy growing right in the middle of my garden. I was so proud of it. It was the biggest poppy you've ever seen. It was a real focal point. I knew that it was going to get even bigger as well only somebody stole it before it had the chance to grow anymore!

I saw it was gone as soon as I walked into my garden. There was a tall stem where my flower had been, but there was nothing on the top.

I could have cried if iron golems were able to cry.

I looked around at the rest of my flowers and I realized that this wasn't the first time someone had stolen from me. I hadn't noticed sooner because the thief had been cunning enough to take them from the back of plants so you couldn't see that they were gone. This time, there was no mistaking the fact that someone had been coming into my garden and helping themselves to my beautiful flowers.

Clearly they were becoming more reckless. All I can say is that they'd better hope that I don't catch them picking my flowers. I spend all my days patrolling the village borders trying to keep it safe and this is how they repay me!

It's enough to make an iron golem want to go off and find some creepers or zombies to bring back to the village. Let the villagers see how it feels to lose the things that they care about.

Once I had the idea that I should punish the village, I couldn't shake it, so I stomped off in the direction of the hills. I was determined to walk as far as it took to find some monsters that were looking for a village to prey on.

Once I was away from the village, I lost my sense of direction and I didn't know where I was going. I walked for what seemed like forever without finding any monsters, not even after the sun had gone down.

Where's a skeleton when you need one?

Day 3

It's amazing what a night sleeping rough will do to change your mind. When I calmed down, I knew that I couldn't set a horde of monsters loose on the village.

It wasn't that I suddenly cared about what the villagers thought. Why should I care about them when they don't care about me?

No, the reason why I decided against leading an army against the village was because the other iron golems would never forgive me for hurting our employers and, believe me, you don't want to get on the wrong side of iron golems. I might be strong, but I wouldn't be able to fight all of the others by myself. I'd be iron ingots in no time.

Instead, I decided that I was going to tell the other iron golems what had happened and see if I could get their help to catch the thief. Once we had him, we could get the villagers to punish him. And if they wouldn't, I was sure that I could get all the other iron golems to stop protecting the village until they did something about it.

Let's see how many monsters stay away once word gets out that the iron golems aren't working any more. If the village was defenseless, it would become monster city in no time.

This was a much better plan. Besides, I was getting lonely wandering around the hills by myself. It would take me forever to find enough monsters to attack the village.

I started to walk back the way I thought I'd come from the village, but I was distracted by the sight of some pretty flowers growing in the forest. I decided to gather some plants to put in my garden. They'd replace the ones that had been stolen from me, even if none of them were quite as nice as my biggest bloom.

I spent so long picking flowers that I lost track of time and the sun was setting by the time I was done. I sat under a tree and watched the sun go down, its rays casting a warm glow across the fields.

From this distance, the village looked friendly and inviting. Nobody would imagine that there was a nasty thief living there.

Day 4

"Someone has been doing what?"

Humphrey, the leader of the iron golems in our village, looked shocked when I told him about my stolen flower.

"Someone has been stealing flowers from my garden," I repeated. "And by the looks of it, they've been doing it for quite a long time."

"This isn't good." Humphrey shook his head. "The whole relationship between iron golems and villagers is based on trust. If we cannot trust the villagers to respect our property, then they cannot expect us to protect them. We need to report this to the village leader."

"Not yet," I cautioned. "If we go to the villagers, then whoever's doing this will just stop and we'll never know who was doing it. Who knows what they might decide to do instead? I have a better idea. If we set up a trap, then we'll be able to find who is responsible and punish them. That way, everyone will know that you shouldn't mess with iron golems."

"Very well," nodded Humphrey. "What did you have in mind?"

I explained my plan and Humphrey smiled. "Yes, I think that will work nicely."

He went off to tell the other iron golems what was going on, leaving me to plant my newly harvested flowers in my garden. They filled in the gaps left by the thief quite nicely, but they were still no replacement for my lovely large poppy.

Once I'd caught the thief, he'd be sorry he ever thought to steal from an iron golem.

Day 5

Today was the day we put my plan into action. Humphrey took most of the iron golems and led them in patrol on the opposite side of the village to my garden. Anyone coming to my garden would think that there was no one around.

Meanwhile, me, Harry, and Hector disguised ourselves as bushes and hid behind some trees to wait and see if the thief would try his luck.

Have you ever seen an iron golem pretending to be a bush? It's hilarious. Hector looked so funny with twigs stuck to his head! Harry really got into character, waving his arms around as if they were branches in the wind.

We all started joking around, making silly noises that we thought a bush might make if a bush could make noise. We were having so much fun, we almost forgot that we were supposed to be catching a thief.

Snap! I heard the sound of a twig breaking as someone stepped on it.

"Shh! I whispered, my good mood vanishing in an instant as I went onto high alert. "Did you hear that?"

Harry and Hector nodded and we all stood completely still, trying to blend into the background as we waited to see who the thief was.

I couldn't believe my eyes. I watched as a little boy crept into my garden. He looked around to make sure that nobody was looking before bending over to gather some flowers. As he reached out to one of the new plants, I sprang out from my hiding place.

"Stop, thief! Those are my flowers you're picking!"

The boy froze, a terrified expression coming over his face. As I came forward to grab him, he dropped the flowers he'd picked and started running.

Hector, Harry, and I raced after him. "Stop! Thief! Stop in the name of the iron golems!"

The little boy ran even faster.

Luckily for me and unluckily for him, a villager child is no match for an iron golem and it wasn't long before I'd caught up with him.

"Stop! Let me go!" He wriggled and squirmed, trying to get away from my tight grip, but you can't make an iron golem let go once it has caught its target.

"No. You've been stealing from me for a long time and it's time for you to face the consequences."

"I didn't steal! They were just flowers!"

I shook my head. "They were flowers from my garden."

"I didn't know it was your garden! How could I?"

I glared at him. "There's a fence all around and you have to open a gate to get in. And if that wasn't enough for you to realize that you were going into someone else's property, the big sign on the gate that says "Harvey the Iron Golem's garden" should have told you."

The boy blushed and looked at his feet. "You're right. I did see the sign and I did know that it was your garden."

"There! The boy admits that he's guilty. Let's take him to the village leader for punishment." Harry started marching off towards the village leader's house.

Pulling the boy's arm, I started to follow him.

"Wait!" cried the boy. "You can't take me to see Jeff. My Grandma would be so upset with me."

"You should have thought of that before you took my flowers." I had no sympathy for him.

Then he started crying. I hate it when children cry. The noise hurts my ears and they look so sad.

"Don't cry, little boy. You now know that you shouldn't steal from the iron golems."

"I know that," sobbed the boy, "but if I get into trouble with Jeff, my Grandma will be so upset with me. She's not very well and if I'm in trouble, it might make her even sicker. That's who the flowers were for. I was just trying to cheer up my Grandma."

"Don't worry about that, Harvey," Hector advised. "That's still no excuse for him to steal from you."

I looked down at the tear stained face of the little boy. "What's your name?"

"Felix," he sniffed.

"All right, Felix. Here's the deal. I won't take you to the village leader if you come and work for me in my garden to make good all the damage you did."

"OK." Felix smiled and I smiled back.

"You're going to regret that," warned Hector as Felix ran off home.

"Maybe." Only time would tell.

Day 6

Felix was already waiting for me by the time I arrived at my garden. "What took you so long?" he chirped.

"Some of us have to work you know," I sniffed. "But don't worry. You'll soon discover what work really means by the time I've finished with you."

I tried to look threatening, but Felix just grinned. He knew I wasn't going to do anything to him.

"All right then. Start over here. See these plants?"

Felix nodded.

"These are weeds. I don't want them here. They'll overpower my flowers. I need you to pull them all out. But make sure you don't pull out any of my flowers. I really will get angry if you do."

"These are the weeds. These are the flowers." Felix pointed to the wrong plants, but when I was about to tell him off, he poked his tongue out at me and I knew he was just joking.

This Felix kid was surprisingly good fun.

We both started gardening. I stood over Felix for a little while, watching to make sure that he was doing what I'd told him to do, but it was soon clear that Felix knew exactly what I needed. I left him to it and went over to another section I wanted to rearrange a bit.

I started digging up plants, dividing them up and placing them where I was planning to replant them.

"What's it like being an iron golem?"

I looked over at Felix. "I thought you were supposed to be weeding."

"I can weed and talk. Why? Can't you? I thought iron golems were supposed to be really cool."

I raised my eyebrows. "What makes you say that?"

"Well, you get to fight anything coming into the village and you're so strong. You could probably knock down a building with just your fists. Crash! Bang!" He pretended he was an iron golem destroying a house.

"I probably could," I nodded, "but I wouldn't. Iron golems are meant to protect villages, not destroy them."

"If I were an iron golem, I'd protect my Grandma and she'd never get sick." Felix appeared to be matter of fact, but the words caught in his throat.

"I'm sorry to hear about your Grandma."

Felix shrugged and turned his attention back to his weeding. "How's this?"

I went over and looked at the patch where he was working. I was amazed to see he'd already cleared the patch I'd given to him. "That's great. Just how I want it."

"So I can go home now?"

I laughed. "That was one tiny section of my garden. Now you've got the rest to do!" I gestured to my other flower beds.

Felix groaned, making me laugh again. He was learning the hard way that crime doesn't pay.

Day 7

When I'd finished my patrol duties, I went over to my garden to find Felix waiting for me already. "Hi, Harvey. See anything interesting on patrol today?"

"Oh yes. This morning I had to stop a fight between two of the wolves and then this afternoon, zombies shuffled into the village, so I had to help them shuffle back out again."

"Really?" Felix's eyes were as wide as saucers.

"Fooled you!" It was my turn to poke my tongue out at him, making Felix giggle. "No, absolutely nothing interesting happened. It never does. You should know that. You've been living here your whole life."

"Yeah, but I've been looking after my Grandma most of the time. I don't get to go out much."

The lad looked so dejected that I wanted to give him a hug, but I didn't want to get too close to him. He was still being punished after all. However, he was such good company, it was hard to stay angry with him and there was a part of me that felt that he'd done enough already to make up for the loss of my flowers.

"Well, you're here now, so enjoy the sunshine and I'll teach you a bit about the flowers you picked."

I started explaining to Felix how different flowers needed to be looked after in different ways. He soaked up all the information. The boy was a fast learner that was for sure.

"Felix! Felix!"

Someone was calling his name. Felix looked at me, panicked. "Oh no! That's my mom. I should have been home for dinner by now. She's going to be so mad with me."

"I'll come with you," I said on the spur of the moment. "I'll tell your mom that you were helping me, which you were. She doesn't need to know that it's because you stole from me."

"Really? You'd do that for me? Thanks, Harvey."

Impulsively, he leaned forward and gave me a hug. I patted him gently on the head. "You're a good friend," he whispered.

"Come on. Let's get you back home." I felt all warm inside. Iron golems didn't really have friends. We worked together and we worked for villagers, but we didn't have friends.

Having a friend felt good.

Day 8

I can't stop thinking about Felix's Grandma. When I took him back to his home, his mom had rushed out to say thank you. "I was so worried," she told me, frantic. "I don't know what we'd do if we lost our Felix."

"That's all right, ma'am. In fact, I must admit that it's my fault that Felix is late back. He came over to help me with my flower garden. We got so caught up in learning about the different plants that we lost track of time. So please don't be cross with him. Be cross with me."

"Oh, I couldn't be cross with you," smiled Felix's mom. "If Felix is with you, then he's safe and that's all that matters to me, especially with his Grandma being sick."

"Felix told me that she was unwell. Is there anything I can do for her?"

"We really need a potion of healing, but we haven't been able to trade for one. If we don't get a potion soon, I don't know what's going to happen. Felix and his Grandma are very close."

"Felix told me that he's been bringing flowers to his Grandma."

"Yes. Flowers are one of the few things that brighten up his Grandma's day. He brought her an enormous red poppy the other day. It's still in a vase on her window sill and she smiles every time she looks at it."

I glanced at Felix and he blushed, but I didn't tell his mom where the flower came from. "Well Felix is welcome to take flowers to his Grandma any time he likes."

I don't know what made me make the offer, but the moment I said it, I knew it was the right thing to do.

"That's very kind of you. You're a good friend to Felix." The smile on his mom's face brightened my day.

I had no idea that his Grandma was so ill though. I feel really bad for Felix. I know how much he loves her.

Day 9

"You didn't have to tell mom that I could take flowers from your garden," Felix told me when he came to see me the next day. "I know you were just being nice to her."

"I know I didn't, but I meant it. I could see how worried your mom is about your Grandma and if a few flowers make things a little easier, then you're more than welcome to them."

"Thanks, Harvey. You're the best!"

The little boy threw his arms around me and squeezed tight before turning to start working in the garden. I had a funny feeling that he was trying not to cry.

"Listen, Felix. I've been thinking."

"Yes?"

"Your mom told me that you need a potion of healing for your Grandma, but you haven't been able to get one."

"No." Felix shook his head. "We've asked every passing Minecraftia if they'd trade. We've even offered them emeralds, but nobody will give us a potion. They all say that they're too valuable and they need them."

"Well I was wondering whether you'd like it if I went out of the village to find a potion for you?"

Felix gasped and his eyes widened. "You'd do that? For me?"

"For your Grandma, yes."

Felix thought for a moment. "I'm sorry, but I can't let you do that."

"Why not? I thought you'd be pleased."

"I am. I want you to go out and get a potion of healing. It's just that I'm not going to let you go alone. I'm going to come with you."

"You?"

This was not part of my plan.

"Yes, me. Everyone knows that iron golems have a terrible sense of direction. If you go by yourself, you'll end up wandering around in circles. If I come along, I'll make sure that you don't get lost."

I had to admit that Felix made sense. "But you're just a kid! I can't take you with me. Not without your mom's permission."

"She'll never say yes. But if you don't take me with you, you'll never be able to find a potion and if we don't get a potion, then my Grandma's going to get worse. You don't have a choice. You have to take me with you."

I looked at him and sighed. He was right.

"OK. You can come with me. But we'll have to plan it carefully so we can get back quickly. Your mom will really worry."

"I know, but I'll write her a letter explaining what we're doing. When she sees the potion, she'll forgive us."

I wasn't so sure, but I could see that Felix's mind was made up and I had to admit that the thought of the little boy keeping me company while we went off to fetch a potion was very appealing.

"All right then young man. You've got yourself a deal."

Day 10

"I got this great book on potion making from the library." Felix came running over to show me his find. "It tells you everything you need to make a potion of healing. We won't have to go out of the village after all. We can just make one!"

I had a funny feeling that if it was that easy, his mom would have mixed up a potion a long time ago. Opening the book, I soon saw that I was right. "Felix, have you read this book?"

Felix shrugged. "I've looked at some of the pictures. I haven't had time to read it properly."

"There are a lot of ingredients we're going to need that we just don't have and I don't think we'll be able to trade for them."

"Like what?"

"Well there's glistering melon for a start."

"What's that?"

I flicked through the pages to find out. "Melon combined with gold, apparently."

"I have melon at home! We're half way there already!"

"Yes, but we still need to add gold to it. Do you have gold at home?"

Felix pouted. "No."

"Then there's all the equipment. Brewing stand, cauldron, potion… I've never seen anything like that in the village. Have you?"

"No," Felix admitted.

I turned back to the pages about potion of healing and read on. "Oh no."

"What?"

I shut the book. "Don't worry about it. We'll just think of another way of getting a potion of healing."

"No, we won't! What is it that you're so worried about?"

He lunged for the book, but I held it up high so he couldn't reach it. Felix jumped up to try and get the book back, but he didn't have a chance. Iron golems are tall and we can stay in the same position for hours if we need to.

"Please, give me the book." Felix started crying.

"All right, then." I handed him the book and he flicked through the pages, trying to find out what had got me so worried.

"Nether Wart." He looked at me, eyes wide. "But that means…"

"Yes. We'll have to go into the Nether. And if we want to make the potion of healing really effective, we'll need to get some Glowstone dust too."

"I don't care. I'm going to do whatever it takes to make my Grandma better."

I had to admire the youth's determination, but I had no idea how we were going to get out of the village, let alone into the Nether.

Day 11

Felix and I sat in my garden, plotting. "Are you really sure that you want to do this?" I asked him. "Villagers aren't supposed to leave the village. You could get into a lot of trouble. We could get into a lot of trouble."

"I don't care. Once we bring back that potion, nobody will stay mad at us."

I wished that I had his confidence. Maybe he was right. Maybe nobody would stay mad at him. I was an iron golem and things were different for me. Part of the iron golem code was that iron golems never deserted their job. I was supposed to be working in the village for at least another year. Leaving, even if it was to assist a villager, was going to get me into hot water with the other iron golems. They might even decide to exile me. I'd be doomed to wander Minecraftia with no friends to keep me company and no garden to help me relax.

Looking at Felix's eager face, I knew that I couldn't let him down. We were going to travel into the Nether and we were going to bring back the ingredients to save Felix's Grandma. If that meant that the iron golems didn't want me around anymore, so be it.

Day 12

Felix met me in my garden just before sunset with a backpack full of supplies.

"I'm so excited! I've been really excited all day! Are you excited?"

I chuckled. "Probably not as much as you are."

"I've left mom a note, but I've put it somewhere so she won't find it until we're too far away for them to stop us."

"Even so, we'd better get a move on. Don't worry. I'll keep you safe."

"I'm not worried," Felix reassured me. "I've got you with me! Nothing's going to hurt me with you around."

"OK. Have you got the book about potion making?"

"I have." Felix patted his backpack.

"Have you got some food?"

"Check!"

"Let's get going then. The sooner we leave, the sooner we'll get back with that potion."

My garden was near the southern edge of the village, so we headed off south, wanting to be clear of the border before Felix was supposed to be in a shelter for the night.

"I've been thinking that we should start by gathering gold," Felix said. "I brought some melon with me, but it won't keep for long. Once we've covered it with gold, it'll last forever!"

"Good plan. There's a mine not far from the village. It shouldn't take us long to get there and I can make you a shelter to keep you safe tonight."

"Thanks, Harvey. You're the best iron golem in the whole wide world!"

Day 13

We managed to reach the mines not long after the sun went down and before any monsters came out, so I found a small cavern for us to take shelter in and quickly put some blocks in the doorway to keep Felix safe.

He was far too agitated to sleep, so it's a good thing that iron golems don't need sleep either. He was a never-ending source of questions. "Do you think we'll find lots of gold? Do you think we should mine more gold than we need? Do you think we could trade the gold for emeralds? Do you think my Grandma would like some emeralds? Do you think it will be easy to get the gold? Do you think the gold is going to be heavy?"

It was exhausting!

At last it was morning and I took the blocks away from the doorway. We headed deeper into the mine, looking for gold. "Is that gold?" Felix rushed forward to a vein.

"No, that's iron." I'd know it anywhere! "But we should take some to upgrade our pickaxe. We need an iron pickaxe if we're going to get some gold."

I pounded into the wall and soon had enough iron to transform our pickaxe. Felix hopped impatiently from one foot to the other as he waited for me to make an iron pickaxe.

"Are you done yet? Are you done yet? Are you done yet?"

At last I nodded.

"Right. Let's find some ore." He raced ahead, going deeper in the mine, forcing me to jog to keep up with him.

"I had no idea there were so many different types of ore!" exclaimed Felix as he pointed out raw metal only to be disappointed when I had to tell him that it wasn't gold. "It's going to take us forever to find the gold we need."

"No it's not," I beamed. "Look over there."

Felix turned to see the wall I was pointing to. Gold!

I started pounding at the wall to make it easier for Felix while he used the iron pickaxe to mine the gold. At last, he had enough gold and I put it in my bag. It was far too heavy for the boy to carry.

"We'll need to smelt it before we can make the glistering melon. We could do it at the blacksmith shop in town, but we can't go back until we have all the other ingredients."

"But I want to take the potion back, not the ingredients to make a potion," protested Felix. "If we don't, we might get into trouble and then we won't have the chance to make the potion and my Grandma won't get better."

"Good point." I thought for a moment. "All right. Our only other option is to see if we can find a Minecraftian and ask them to smelt the gold for us. Good idea, we mined more than we needed – we can use the leftover mine to pay for their furnace."

"Sounds like a plan!"

Day 14

Felix was in a really good mood now that we had one of the ingredients. "This is going to be easy!"

I wasn't so sure. The gold had been easy to get, but that was just one ingredient. Everything else was going to be much harder.

"Let's go to the Nether," suggested Felix.

"Not just yet," I cautioned. I still wasn't sure that it would be a good idea to take Felix into the Nether. He wouldn't last five minutes against the monsters by himself and I was just one iron golem. What would happen if he fell into the lava while I was battling zombie pigmen? "Let's find a witch's hut first."

"All right. But I'm really looking forward to going into the Nether. I was reading all about it in the library."

He started telling me all about the kinds of things we might find in the Nether, but I wasn't really listening to him. The more I thought about it, the more I wished that I'd left him back in the village. What had I been thinking, bringing a child on a dangerous quest like this?

Day 15

"We've been walking for hours! When are we going to get there?"

"It hasn't been hours and we'll get there when we get there."

I didn't mean to be cross with Felix and I could see that my harsh words had upset him a little, so I picked him up and put him on my shoulders as we walked along so that he could rest for a while. We'd decided that we were going to find a witch's hut next, but although we knew that they spawned in swamps, we had no idea where to find a swamp. We also had no idea if there would be a hut inside one once we did.

"What's that over there?" Felix tapped me on the shoulder to get my attention, pointing off in the distance.

I peered in the direction he'd indicated and saw what looked like a person coming towards us.

"It must be a Minecraftian. Let's go and see if they know where a witch's hut is."

We headed towards the person and sure enough, it was a traveling Minecraftian.

"Hello!" Felix waved at him once we were in shouting distance.

"Hello!" The Minecraftian waved back. "You're a long way from home. I never expected an iron golem and a villager child to be so far away from a village."

"We're on a mission," announced Felix proudly. "We're gathering ingredients to make a potion of healing."

"Really?" The Minecraftian looked impressed. "Most villagers don't know anything about potion making."

"We have a book that tells us everything we need to do. It doesn't look too tricky."

"Shh!" The Minecraftian looked from side to side. "Don't say that or all the villagers will figure out how to do it!" He winked at Felix, making him laugh. "Still, gathering all those ingredients can be dangerous. Are you sure you're up to the task?"

"That's why I brought my best friend with me." Felix patted my shoulder.

"We were wondering if you knew of any witch's huts around here." I decided that it was time I did a bit of talking. Much as the Minecraftian could help us, I didn't completely trust him, so I wanted to remind him just how powerful an iron golem could be in case he tried to steal from us.

"Witch's huts?" The Minecraftian thought for a moment, a frown wrinkling his forehead. "No, I can't say that I do. There's a swamp back there. Maybe you'll find a witch's hut. I do know where a portal to the Nether is though."

"A portal to the Nether?" Felix and I gasped.

"Yes." The Minecraftian nodded. "It's just on top of that hill over there. I used it this morning. You'll need to be careful though. There are a lot of monsters down there. It's not very safe."

"That's all right. Harvey will protect me."

I didn't say anything. If there were a lot of monsters, I really didn't want Felix coming down with me.

"We were wondering," Felix said. "We just mined a heap of gold ore. We need to smelt it into ingots so that we can make a glistering melon. Would you be able to help us?"

The Minecraftian looked at him.

"You can keep any leftover gold. We have loads. Show him, Harvey!"

I opened up my back and showed the Minecraftian just how much gold we'd mined.

He whistled. "That is a lot of gold. All right. You've got yourself a deal." He glanced up at the sky. "We haven't got long before the sunset though. Why don't we build a quick shelter and then I can smelt your gold safely? It should all be done by morning."

"Good idea."

Working with the Minecraftian, we soon had a shelter up. It wasn't the best shelter Minecraftia had ever seen, but it would do to keep us safe overnight and I would stay awake to watch over Felix and our gold ingots.

We finished just as the sun was setting and Felix went straight into the shelter to go to sleep.

"OK," the Minecraftian said to me. "I'll get the gold smelting started and then I'm going to get some rest as well – that's if you don't mind staying up to keep an eye on things?"

"I don't mind at all."

The Minecraftian curled up in a corner of the shelter and was soon snoring, leaving me to watch over the furnace and think about how I was going to keep Felix out of the Nether.

Day 16

The Minecraftian was up bright and early the next morning. Going over to the furnace, he pulled out a load of gold nuggets.

"There you go," he said, passing them over to me. "You need eight gold nuggets to make a glistering melon, so I'm giving you sixteen, just in case."

"And the rest of the gold is yours to keep," I told him. "Thank you for smelting the gold for us. You've saved us a lot of work."

"Any time," the Minecraftian smiled. "And best of luck with your potion. I hope you manage to find all your ingredients."

He set off on his travels, leaving me to wake up Felix.

"Come on, Felix. Time to get up. We've got a witch to find!"

Felix yawned and stretched. "Where's the Minecraftian?"

"He's gone," I replied, "but he's given us all the gold nuggets we need, plus a few spare, so we can make a couple of glistering melons."

"Let's do that now," Felix decided. "I don't know how much longer the melon will last."

The Minecraftian had left his crafting table behind, so we put the melon in the middle surrounded by the gold nuggets.

"Wow," breathed Felix. "That's amazing!"

Sitting in the middle of the crafting table was a glistering melon.

Felix picked it up. "It's really heavy. And look how beautiful it is!"

He held it up to the light, admiring the way it sparkled in the sun. "We're one step closer to making a healing potion. Come on. Time to visit the swamp. We're going to find a witch today, I just know we are."

Day 17

We did not find a witch yesterday. We spent all day wandering around in the swamp getting wet and muddy for nothing. There was no sign of a witch.

What was even worse was that we didn't have a shelter for Felix, so I made him sleep underneath a bush. It wouldn't protect him if a monster saw him, but maybe they wouldn't notice him tucked away like that.

I rested against a tree next to the bush, keeping my eyes open for any threats.

"What have we here?"

Standing in the middle of the clearing was a witch. I could have sworn that she wasn't there a moment ago. I could have kicked myself for letting her sneak up on me.

She moved closer. "An iron golem. We don't get many of your sort around here. I could do with a new servant. You're coming home with me."

She beckoned me over. "Come on. You're an iron golem with no master. You have to obey my commands."

What she was saying was true. An iron golem with no master was open to any offer, no matter who was making it. However, what she didn't know was that I had a master. Felix. And I was bound to protect him, no matter what.

I pretended to go with the witch, but as soon as I got close enough, I unleashed a powerful punch.

Whack!

"Ow!" screeched the witch. "What did you do that for?"

I didn't waste any energy replying, hitting her again as hard as I could.

"Now I see why you're out in the wilderness. You're a rogue iron golem. Well, I know just what to do with your sort." She reached into her robe to pull out a potion. I couldn't let her use it, so I knocked it out of her hand making it smash against a tree.

"No!" the witch cried. "That was my last potion of healing!"

That had been a potion of healing? Now I was really mad. If I'd been a little more careful, I could have taken the potion from the witch and Felix could have gone home.

I ran at the witch, whirling my fists. She put up her hands to defend herself, but she didn't stand a chance. With a final blow, I knocked her out and she disappeared in a puff of smoke, leaving behind a little pile of glowstone dust.

I might not have been able to get a potion of healing from the witch, but at least I had another ingredient.

Day 18

Felix slept through the entire fight with the witch, so when he woke up, he was amazed to see that I had the glowstone dust. "Where did you get that from?" he gasped.

"From the witch that attacked me last night," I replied. "And you know what a witch means."

"There's a witch's hut nearby," nodded Felix. "We have to find it!"

"We will. It can't be far."

We set off into the swamp.

"Which direction did the witch come from?"

I was embarrassed to have to admit that I didn't know. "She just appeared."

"Should we split up and look in different places? We might cover more ground that way."

Me? Let Felix loose in the swamp by himself? I don't think so!

"I think we should stick together. If you sit on my shoulders, you should be able to see further. That will give us the best chance of finding the witch's hut."

"Good idea!" Felix climbed up onto my shoulders and we made our way slowly through the swamp, keeping our eyes open for the witch's hut.

"Over there! I see it!" Felix whooped in happiness.

Sure enough, there was the witch's hut.

Felix got down from my shoulders and we both stood there, relieved to have finally found it. I didn't know what we would have done if we hadn't.

"Come on. Let's go inside and see what we can find."

Felix raced up to the hut. He stopped in the doorway, looking back at me to see why I hadn't followed him.

"What's wrong? Why aren't you coming inside?"

"Look at the size of me. Now look at the size of the hut."

"Oh."

I was far too big to fit into the little hut.

"It's fine. You go inside and see what supplies the witch has. It's perfectly safe now that the witch has gone."

Felix headed into the hut. "Oh wow!" I heard him cry from inside. "There's so much cool stuff in here! She's got most of the things we need just lying around – a cauldron, brewing stand, bottles."

"See if you can find anything else," I suggested. "Maybe she might have some Nether wart or even a potion of healing."

I knew that the witch had said that she'd broken her last one, but maybe she'd left another potion of healing in her hut.

At last, Felix came out of the hut. "This is all I can find."

He held his hands out to me and I could see fermented spider eye, pufferfish, golden carrots, and gunpowder but no Nether wart.

"Oh well. Let's camp here for the night and tomorrow we can go to the Nether portal the Minecraftian told us about. We've almost got everything we need. Not long now and we've got the potion of healing for your grandmother."

Felix smiled and went back into the witch hut to settle down for the night. "Good night, Harvey! I couldn't have done this without you."

Day 19

As soon as the sun rose, Felix came running out of the witch's hut. "Come on, Harvey. Time to go. We need to get to the Nether portal."

"All right, Felix. Before we leave, could you just go into the witch's hut and have a look one last time to see if there's anything else that we need?"

"I've already looked. We've got everything useful."

"Check once more. Just for me."

I gave him my best pleading look. It's not great. Iron golems can't really move their faces all that much, but it must have done the trick because he huffed and stomped back into the hut.

Quick as a flash, I went up the stairs and shut the door behind him, jamming it shut with a tree branch.

"Hey! What are you doing? Let me out!" Felix banged on the door, but it was locked fast.

"I'm sorry, Felix, but I can't take you into the Nether with me. I just can't risk it. You'll be perfectly safe in the witch's hut. There's plenty of food and water there and no monsters will dare go into the hut because they won't know the witch isn't there. Sit tight and I'll come for you as soon as I can. We can make the potion together."

"Harvey! Don't leave me!"

I turned my back and walked away, trying not to let Felix see how upset I was that I had to do this to him. I was really going to miss the little guy.

Day 20

Iron golems have a terrible sense of direction. Everybody knows it. It was why I'd agreed to let Felix come along on our mission in the first place. He'd been the one to make sure we didn't get lost and he'd done a great job.

Why was I stupid enough to think that I could manage without him?

I could have sworn that the Minecraftian had said that the Nether portal was just over the hill, but I'd walked all the way to the closest hill and it was nowhere to be seen. I was standing right at the top of the hill, so if it was here, I would see it.

I gazed around and despaired at how many hills I could see in the area. That was just on this side of the swamp. What happened if I'd come to the wrong side? I could be in completely the wrong place and I'd never know. I couldn't be gone for too long. I'd left Felix with plenty of food, but it wasn't going to last forever.

I had no idea what to do.

I'd heard that you could build Nether portals, but I had no idea where to start and gathering the resources would take time. That was time that I didn't have.

There was nothing else to do. I started walking towards the next hill, hoping that I would eventually remember where it was the Minecraftian had told me to go.

Do you know how long it takes to go up and down hills? A long time. And it's boring. If you've seen one hill, you've seen them all. If Felix was with me, he'd probably be talking about how great the views were from the hilltops, but I didn't care about how pretty it was. I needed to get to the Nether if we were going to save his Grandma.

Night fell and I still hadn't found the Nether portal. This was where it was a good thing that I'd left Felix back at the witch's hut. If he was with me, we'd have to stop and find somewhere safe for him to sleep. I could take care of myself and I didn't need to sleep.

I kept marching through the night, determined to find the way to the Nether no matter what it took.

Day 21

When it was midday and I still hadn't found the portal, I started to worry. If I didn't find it soon, I'd have to go and get Felix and risk taking him into the Nether with me.

Suddenly, a strange noise caught my attention. It sounded as though someone, no, a whole group of someones were whimpering and crying. It was most disturbing.

A feeling of panic came over me. Was Felix crying? Had someone taken him from the witch's hut?

"Don't worry, Felix! I'm coming to save you!" I yelled, as I charged in the direction of the noise, but when I saw what was causing all the commotion, I stopped in my tracks.

It was the Nether portal.

Although I'd never seen one before, it wasn't hard to recognize. A black obsidian door frame stood on the top of the hill, a strange purple glow coming from inside it. As I drew closer, I could see what looked like purple snowflakes whirring around inside. I put my hand in to catch one and pulled it out again quickly. My hand felt very peculiar, all tingly.

I had to be brave. It didn't matter how odd it felt, I needed to go through the portal to get to the Nether.

I closed my eyes and counted to three. One, two, three!

Stepping into the Nether portal felt as though I was falling forward, but when I opened my eyes, my feet were still firmly on the ground.

However, the ground was very different to the Overworld. I'd made it. I was in the Nether.

According to the book about potions, Nether wart only grew in fortresses, so that's what I needed to find. A fortress would be huge. How hard could finding one be?

Day 22

I had no idea finding a fortress in the Nether would be so difficult. It's so confusing down here. If my sense of direction was bad in the Overworld, it's even worse down here. I have no idea where I am or where the Nether portal I used is.

It all looks the same to me. The walls are dark, light coming from lava streams. And the lava is so hot! I could feel myself almost melting into iron ingots the closer I got. I'm going to have to be careful not to be knocked into it. I'd never get out alive.

As I was edging my way around a lake full of lava, I heard a peculiar sound. It was a bit like a pig, but not a pig I'd ever encountered.

Zombie pigmen!

I'd heard of them before. I wasn't too worried, but if they ganged up on me, then it would be tough to fight them and if there were too many, I was bound to lose.

I tried to creep away as quietly as possible, but when I turned a corner, thinking I'd escaped without being seen, I came face to face with a zombie pigman!

I gulped. "Er… hello?"

"Oink-grunt."

He hadn't attacked me immediately. This was a good sign.

"I don't suppose you know if there are any fortresses around here?"

"Oink-grunt." Was that a yes or a no?

"Well, would you mind letting me past at least?"

"Oink-grunt."

The zombie pigman stared at me for a moment and I braced myself to fight. Then it stepped aside, letting me go past without a fight.

Maybe the Nether isn't as bad as people say it is.

Day 23

I finally found a Nether fortress. I stood outside, looking up at the entrance. It was a formidable building and strong as I am, even I was nervous about what I might find.

However, there was one thing that I knew I would find that I really needed: Nether wart. This was it. The final ingredient for Felix's Grandma's potion of healing.

I walked up to the gate and pushed it open. I was standing at the edge of a large courtyard. The walls were black, the floor was black, and everywhere around me was black. The only light came from torches dotted about.

It was quiet. Too quiet.

I couldn't see any Nether wart lying around, but then again that would be too easy.

I stepped into the courtyard, wondering which to go first. There were some steps leading up to a door, so I decided to see what was in that room.

I tiptoed up the stairs trying not to make any noise. I didn't want to attract any monsters.

I put my hand on the door. It felt warm. Hopefully it wouldn't open onto more lava.

I took a deep breath and opened the door. When I saw what was on the other side, I froze.

Blazes!

They seemed as stunned to see me as I was to see them. Once the surprise wore off, they came charging towards me, blasting fireballs.

I had a split second to decide what to do. If I shut the door and ran away, they'd come after me, but they'd be in the open courtyard. I'd be surrounded.

I decided to stand my ground and fight back. I had a little more control over how many could attack if I stayed where I was.

The blazes were harder to fight than anything I'd ever encountered and there were so many of them I lost count. I wanted to give up, but I could hear Felix talking to me, telling me how brave I am, how strong I am, that I was the only chance he had of curing his Grandma.

Thinking of Felix gave me extra strength and I charged forward, knocking the blazes flying. I was like a mad iron golem, fists flying, my attack so fast and powerful that the blazes didn't stand a chance.

56

After what seemed like forever, the fight was finally over, blazes lying on the ground all around me. I had a few scrapes myself. My health was lower than it had ever been. The worst thing I'd ever had to fight in the village was a few zombies and then I'd had other iron golems with me. Now I was on my own and the monsters were tougher than anything I'd ever encountered.

There was no time to waste. I had to find some Nether wart.

There was a door opposite the one I'd come through and I walked over. This time, I was more careful before opening it. I tried to listen to see if I could hear any monsters on the other side.

Silence.

Slowly, I opened the door. The corridor behind it was empty, ending in another door. Once again, I listened before going through.

This time, I could hear something. I opened the door a tiny crack and peeped through to see a group of skeletons milling around. They didn't look anything like any skeletons I'd ever seen before. They had swords instead of bows and I realized that they must be wither skeletons.

There was no way I was going to run into the room to attack them. I'd suffered too much damage at the hands of the blazes. But watching them, I had an idea. I nipped back to the room where I'd found the blazes and picked up a few resources.

I yanked the door open. "Hey, skeletons! It's an all you can eat iron golem buffet standing right here!"

I waved my arm through the door, hoping to attract their attention. Sure enough, they came racing towards me.

I ducked back and put an extra block in the doorway, using the resources I'd gathered. The skeletons tried to come through, but they were too big and I was able to hit them every time they came near me. They were too stupid to stop attacking and soon there was a big pile of bones lying in the doorway where the skeletons had been.

Removing the block, I went through to the room and spotted a chest in the corner. Going over, I opened it up.

Nether wart! Just what I'd been looking for. I gathered it up and headed back the way I came as quickly as I could. I'd been lucky to survive this long in the fortress. I didn't want to stay any longer than I had to in case more monsters came along.

Day 24

Although I found my way out of the fortress easily enough, getting out of the Nether was a different story. Once again, my sense of direction deserted me and it took me ages to find the Nether portal that I'd used. It seemed like forever before I finally found the way out and at last, I was standing on top of the hill where I'd left the Overworld. Although, judging by the position of the sun, it was more like a few hours.

Even though I'd only been gone a couple of days, it felt very strange to be back in my realm. The sun seemed even brighter than I remembered, the birdsong a welcome change from the eerie sounds that haunted the Nether. I never wanted to go back to that place and I was glad that Felix hadn't been there with me.

Felix. I needed to get back to him as soon as possible so we could make the potions. The hard part was going to be finding the witch's hut again. I was sure that it was off to the west of the swamp, but maybe it was to the east.

I chose a direction at random and started walking. At least I knew that the hut was in the swamp, which was going to be easier to explore than going up and down hills all day. I'd get back to him soon enough.

Day 25

"Felix? Are you there?"

I stood outside the witch's hut. The branch that I'd used to block the door was gone and Felix was nowhere to be seen.

A cold knot of fear tightened in the pit of my stomach. What had happened? Had skeletons come and taken him away? Had zombies broken down the door to get to him? It was almost night. If he wasn't in the witch's hut, he'd be in danger.

"Felix? Felix!" I rushed around the clearing, calling his name. Where could he be?

I didn't know what to do. What if I walked off in one direction to find him and he'd been taken the opposite way? I'd never find him and he'd never know that I had the Nether wart for him.

"So you came back then." Felix emerged from the bushes, carrying some fish. "It's about time."

He walked up to the hut, leaving me outside.

"Felix! I was so worried about you." A huge wave of relief washed over me. "I thought you'd been eaten by monsters. How did you get the branch away?"

"It took me ages," he admitted. "I tried all sorts of things to move it. I shoved the door, I kicked the door, I tried to catch it with some rope through the window, but nothing worked and eventually I gave up. I was so mad at you for leaving me. But after a good night's sleep, I'd calmed down and I realized that you were only trying to protect me so I forgave you. We're still best friends."

He smiled up at me.

"I'm glad to hear it, but that still doesn't explain how you got out."

"Well, I spent the morning sitting on the witch's bed, bored. But then I noticed something strange on the floor. When I looked closer, I discovered a trap door! I opened it and there were a whole heap more potions. No healing potions, but there was a potion of strength. I drank it and it gave me enough strength to be able to push the door open.

"But that wasn't the only thing I found. Wait here."

He dashed up the stairs into the hut and returned a moment later with a potion.

I looked at it, stunned. "A potion of regeneration," I breathed.

"A potion of regeneration," nodded Felix. "If we give it to Grandma after the potion of healing, she's going to be well in no time."

"That's great news!"

"So what was the Nether like?" Felix asked.

"You don't want to know," I warned.

"I really do! I still haven't forgiven you for not taking me with you. I really want to know what it was like down there."

"All right," I sighed. "It's dark and dangerous. Monsters lurk behind every corner and if it's not a monster, it's lava and if it's not lava, it's a fire."

"Cool!"

I shook my head. Felix would never know how lucky he was that I'd left him back here.

"Anyway, I got the Nether wart we need, even if I did have to fight off a whole army of blazes to get it."

"A whole army of blazes? What happened?" Felix sat cross legged on the floor as I started telling him all about my adventures in the Nether.

Day 26

First thing in the morning, we gathered together everything we needed to make the potion of healing. "First, we need three bottles of water," I read from the book.

"Not a problem. There's a lake really close to here. I went fishing there every day. I'll be right back."

He dashed off through the trees while I set up the brewing stand.

Soon he was back with the water. "What next?"

I read on. "We put the Nether wart at the top of the brewing stand with the bottles of water underneath."

Felix put the bottles at the bottom with Nether wart on top. We watched as the Nether wart started to trickle down through the stand, bubbling and spluttering as it transformed the water into an awkward potion.

"This is so cool!" Felix was transfixed by the brewing stand, watching as the water became darker with a slight glow.

At last, we had three awkward potions.

"Now we do the same, but with the glistering melon."

Felix put the glistering melon where the Nether wart had been. It glowed before releasing melon juice, trickling down to combine with the awkward potion to turn bright red.

"Finally, add the glowstone dust for extra power."

Carefully, Felix added the glowstone dust and once more, the brewing stand worked its magic.

At last we had three potions of healing. Felix's Grandma was going to be healed!

Day 27

It took so long to brew the potions that we had to spend one last night at the witch's hut, but as soon as the sun rose, we set off in the direction of the village.

"Goodbye witch's hut! I never want to see you again!" called Felix.

"I'm sorry that I had to lock you up in there."

"It's OK. You did the right thing. It would have been hard for you to get the Nether wart if you spent your whole time worrying about me. As long as my Grandma gets better, that's all that matters. Mom is going to be so pleased to see us!"

I hoped that he was right. Now that we were going back to the village, I wondered whether the iron golems would be happy to see me again. After all, I'd deserted my post, even if it was for a good cause. That was the worst thing an iron golem could do.

Felix chattered away, not realizing that I was worried about what was going to happen when we got home. I let him talk, not wanting to ruin his good mood. There was a part of me that wished I was back in the Nether fighting blazes. That would be a lot less frightening than facing Humphrey when he was angry.

"I'd forgotten how far away the village is," remarked Felix after a few hours of walking. "Do you think we're going to get there before the sun goes down?"

"No," I replied. "We'll need to build a shelter for you soon."

"Can't we keep going?" pouted Felix. "I don't mind going without sleep. The sooner we get back to village, the sooner my Grandma can have her potions."

"You won't be able to give her any potions if they get smashed in a fight," I pointed out. "That's what happened to the witch. She had a potion of healing, but it got broken before she could use it. I'd hate to have to go through all of this for nothing."

"All right, but we need to get going again the second the sun rises."

"Of course."

We quickly built a makeshift shelter for Felix out of wood big enough for both of us. "Come on, Harvey. Let's get some rest."

I shook my head. "No. You go in. I'm going to patrol, just to be on the safe side."

"All right, then."

Felix was too tired to argue, so he went into the shelter and closed the door behind him, leaving me with my thoughts of what Humphrey was going to say when I saw him tomorrow.

Day 28

We set off bright and early the next morning and by lunchtime, we could see the village on the horizon. "This is it, Harvey! We're almost home."

He started running, forcing me to run to keep up with him. The closer we came, the more I wanted to run in the opposite direction. Maybe I could leave Felix here to find his own way back and disappear off into Minecraftia.

As soon as I had the thought, I dismissed it. I was an iron golem and my honor was at stake. I'd done what I thought was the right thing and if Humphrey couldn't see that, then I'd accept whatever punishment he thought I deserved.

"Look, Harvey! It's the farms! Hello Farmer Tom!" Felix waved at the farmers as he sped past, missing the comical look of surprise on their faces at the sight of a little villager boy zooming in from Minecraftia.

"Felix? Is that Felix?" The murmur became a roar as news of Felix's return spread through the village like wildfire.

Felix ran down the road towards his home. "Mom! Mom!" he called.

His mom came out of their house, a nervous expression on her face turning to joy as she saw her son. "Felix! Where have you been? We've all been so worried about you."

"I went to get a potion of healing for Grandma. Look!" He reached into his backpack and pulled out the potions we'd made.

"Oh my goodness, Felix. Come inside. We need to get this to your Grandma straight away."

She hurried him into the house, closing the door behind them. I was left out in the street, all alone.

"Harvey. I'm surprised that you've got the nerve to show your face around here."

I whirled round to see Humphrey before me, flanked by the other iron golems. "I've been-"

"I don't care where you've been. You abandoned your post in the village. You have broken our most important law. There is no excuse for what you've done. Lads, take him away. He will face trial tomorrow."

I didn't even try to resist as two of the iron golems stepped forward to grab my arms. Whatever the punishment, as long as Felix' Grandma was better it would all be worth it.

Day 29

I spent the night locked up in the iron golems' shelter. There were at least two iron golems outside my door at all times so that I couldn't try to escape, not that I would. I'd spent all night thinking about how important it was to Felix that he heal his Grandma and I was at peace with whatever the other iron golems decided.

There was a rattle of keys at the door. I stood up as Humphrey came in. "Come on, Harvey. We're all waiting for you."

Obediently, I followed Humphrey out of the room, the iron golem guards falling into step behind us.

He led me outside to where the iron golems were gathered. They parted to let me and Humphrey through and that's when I saw Felix standing there with a big smile on his face.

"Felix! What are you doing here? This is the iron golems' shelter."

"This is a special occasion," Humphrey told me. "We thought it fitting that Felix should be allowed to come in and see you."

Felix stepped forward. "Harvey! My Grandma's better! And it's all thanks to you. Mom told me that she got worse after I left and if we didn't come back when we did, she wouldn't have lasted much longer. Instead, she's out and about and she wants to meet you. Come on, Grandma! Don't be shy!"

An old lady stepped through the iron golems, Felix's mom by her side. "Hello, Harvey," she said. "Felix told me how brave you were and I want to thank you for getting those potions for me."

"It was my pleasure, ma'am."

"I've got something for you." Felix took out the remaining piece of glistering melon. "I'd like you to have this as a little reminder of our adventures together."

I reached forward and took it from his hands. It looked even more sparkly now that we were home. "Thank you, Felix. I will treasure it always."

"And now, Harvey, it's time for your sentence."

I turned to Humphrey. If he exiled me from the village, I would always have my memories.

Humphrey cleared his throat. "Harvey Iron Golem. You are released from your village patrol duties."

I gulped. I knew that this was likely, but hearing Humphrey say the words was still a shock.

"From this moment on," he continued, "you will instead serve Felix and his family."

"What?" I couldn't believe what I was hearing.

"That's right. I hereby sentence you to be Felix's companion forever. You have proven that iron golems are more than just guards. We are true friends to the villagers."

If iron golems could cry, I would have burst into tears of happiness. Instead, I picked up Felix, swinging him round and round in a big hug as all the other iron golems cheered.

Day 30

I looked around my little garden. It was amazing how many weeds could grow in just a few short weeks. My flowers were already being overwhelmed by them.

I set to work, starting to pull out all the unwanted plants.

"Do you need some help?"

I looked up to Felix standing next to me. "Some help would be great."

Felix knelt down beside me and started pulling out weeds. "I've been thinking and I decided that your garden is missing a few things."

I glanced at my flower beds. I loved it just the way it was. "I can't think what. The new plants we put in just before we left are doing really well. You can hardly tell that somebody stole some flowers."

I glared at him, although there was no malice in it.

"You have plenty of flowers," Felix agreed, "but what you don't have is any fruit. I figured that we should grow our own melons so that if we ever need to make any more potions of healing, we will have plenty of fruit, ripe for the plucking."

I nodded slowly. "You're right. This garden could use some melons in it. Where were you thinking of putting it?"

Felix gazed about, thinking. "Right there," he decided finally, pointing to where my beautiful big red poppy had been. "That way, it's right in the middle of the garden so we know exactly where it is."

"Good idea. Let's start preparing the ground."

As we started pulling out plants to make some space for the melon, Felix chatted away, telling me all about how he couldn't walk through the village without somebody wanting to know what had happened on our adventures.

Having a best friend is the greatest feeling in the world.

Printed in Great Britain
by Amazon

78610916R00047